D0943881

DISCARD

Our Basic
FREEDOMS

FREEDOM *of*
THE PRESS

Marysville Public Library
231 S. Plum Street
Marysville, OH 43040
937-642-1876

STEPHANIE HOOVER

Gareth Stevens
PUBLISHING

Please visit our website, www.garethstevens.com.
For a free color catalog of all our high-quality books,
call toll free 1-800-542-2595 or fax 1-877-542-2596.

Cataloging-in-Publication Data
Names: Hoover, Stephanie.
Title: Freedom of the press / Stephanie Hoover.
Description: New York : Gareth Stevens Publishing, 2017. | Series: Our basic freedoms | Includes index.
Identifiers: ISBN 9781482461107 (pbk.) | ISBN 9781482461886 (library bound) | ISBN 9781482461114 (6 pack)
Subjects: LCSH: Freedom of the press--United States--Juvenile literature.
Classification: LCC KF4774.H66 2017 | DDC 342.7308'53--dc23

Published in 2017 by
Gareth Stevens Publishing
111 East 14th Street, Suite 349
New York, NY 10003

Copyright © 2017 Gareth Stevens Publishing

Developed and Produced by Focus Strategic Communications, Inc.
Project Manager: Adrianna Edwards
Editor: Ron Edwards
Layout and Composition: Ruth Dwight, Laura Brady
Copyeditors: Adrianna Edwards, Francine Geraci
Media Researchers: Maria DeCambra, Adrianna Edwards
Proofreader: Francine Geraci
Index: Ron Edwards

Photo Credits: Credit Abbreviations: G Getty Images; LOC Library of Congress; NARA National Archives and
Records Administration; S Shutterstock; WC Wikimedia Commons. Position on the page: T: top, C: center, B:
bottom, L: left, R: right. Cover: Caiaimage/Tom Merton/G; 4: Everett Historical/S; 5: Everett Historical/S; 6:
LOC/LC-USZ62-49739; 7: White House Collection/White House Historical Association; 8: Anton Watman/S; 9:
A katz/S; 10: Everett Historical/S; 11 T: Everett Historical/S; 11 B: Everett Historical/S; 12: Steve Heap/S; 13:
Hot Property/S; 14: Evan El-Amin/S; 15: Stuart Monk/S; 16: J. Bicking/S; 17: Helga Esteb/S; 18: CebotariN/S;
19: Kaspard Grinvalds/S; 20: Photo.ua/S; 21: Rawpixel.com/S; 22: Danny E. Hooks/S; 23: Katherine Welles/S;
24: Everett Historical/S; 25: Kobby Dagan/S; 26: Haak78/S; 28: Bikeriderlondon/S; 29: Helga Esteb/S; 30: Marc
Van Scyoc/S; 31: Christopher Penler/S; 32: A. Aleksandravicius/S; 33: Everett Historical/S; 34: NARA/531443;
35: Orhan Cam/S; 36: © Luigi Novi/WC; 37: Roman Motizov/S; 39: Igor kisselev/S; 40: Goodluz/S; 41: Yulia
Grigoryeva/S; 42: Joseph Sohm/S; 43: Emka74/S; 44: Everett Historical/S; 45: White House Collection/White
House Historical Association.

All rights reserved. No part of this book may be reproduced in any form
without permission from the publisher, except by a reviewer.

Printed in the United States of America
CPSIA compliance information: Batch CW17GS: For further information contact
Gareth Stevens, New York, New York at 1-800-542-2595.

CONTENTS

CHAPTER 1

THE FOUNDING FATHERS AND THE FREE PRESS

THE FOUNDING FATHERS

The First Amendment to the Constitution combines several important protections. Freedom of religion, speech, and assembly are all guaranteed. So is the right to petition the government. But many Founding Fathers felt that, above all else, a free democracy was impossible without a free press. This, too, is guaranteed by the First Amendment.

Fast Fact

THOMAS JEFFERSON

Thomas Jefferson was a strong and consistent supporter of a free press, a stance that persisted even when he was savagely attacked by opposition newspapers during his presidency (1801–1809). It would be difficult to exceed his 1787 statement of support: "Were it left to me to decide whether we should have a government without newspapers or newspapers without government, I should not hesitate a moment to prefer the latter."

THE FIRST NEWSPAPERS

Newspapers were some of the earliest businesses established in the American colonies. They played a crucial role in spreading the word about the American Revolution. Upon winning independence from Great Britain, several states passed laws protecting these publications from government intrusion. In 1791, the **ratification** of the Bill of Rights made freedom of the press a national, federally protected concept. It was not long, though, before this right was tested. One of those challenges came from an unexpected source: the president of the United States.

Fast Fact

GUTENBERG PRINTING PRESS

Around 1440, Johannes Gutenberg (right) invented a machine that allowed metal letters to be moved and rearranged. A finished page was "typeset," meaning there would be no more changes. These letters—called "typeface"—were then covered with ink. The inked letters were literally pressed against paper, creating the term "the press."

SEEDS OF A FREE PRESS

Many of the men and women who first settled in America came from places where the government or church controlled the press. Authorities often prohibited newspapers from reporting the truth. As a result, citizens had limited knowledge of events in their own countries.

During colonial times, the American press was steered by the British. In 1733, printer and journalist John Peter Zenger disagreed with the actions of New York's governor, William Cosby. Cosby was appointed by the king, not elected by New York's citizens. He made many decisions favoring Great Britain rather than New Yorkers. Zenger ridiculed these decisions in his newspaper, *The New York Weekly Journal*.

Cosby had Zenger arrested for "libel," which means publishing false stories. Zenger said that his statements could be proven true and therefore could not be libelous. The jury found him not guilty.

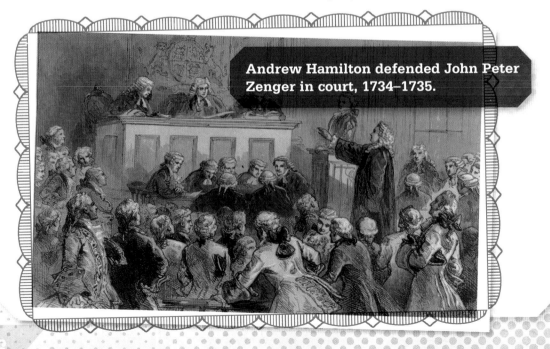

Andrew Hamilton defended John Peter Zenger in court, 1734–1735.

★ ★ ★ ★ ★ ★ ★ ★ ★ ★ ★

PENNSYLVANIA PACKET

The *Pennsylvania Packet* began as a weekly newspaper in 1771. In 1784, it became the first successful daily newspaper in the nation. The paper continued under various names for over 50 years.

SILENCING THE PRESS

Seven years after the passage of the First Amendment, freedom of the press was seriously threatened by an unlikely foe. In 1798, President John Adams pushed the **Alien and Sedition Acts** through Congress. Written, spoken, or published comments that challenged government action or policies were made illegal. Publicly, Adams said the laws protected America's national interest against threats from France. Privately, however, many believed Adams simply wanted to silence the press, which gave voice to his opponents.

Adams's actions outraged the American public. He lost his bid for re-election to Thomas Jefferson, and the Alien and Sedition Acts were repealed.

John Adams's Alien and Sedition Acts resulted in the arrest of 20 newspaper editors.

DANGERS OF A STATE-RUN PRESS

A "free press" is operated and owned by private individuals and companies, not representatives of the ruling authority.

Even today, there are many countries where journalists are forced to print what the government tells them to. In North Korea, for instance, schools are not allowed access to the Internet, and less than 10 percent of the population owns cell phones. China jails more journalists than any other nation in the world. Their crime? Writing stories viewed as "anti-state" by the Chinese government.

The image above of a television announcer without a mouth and the inscription "News" in Korean represents the lack of media freedom in North Korea.

JASON REZAIAN

Working as a journalist in those countries without freedom of the press is a dangerous job. Take the case of American-born Jason Rezaian. In 2008, he and his wife moved to Iran, where he wrote about that country for several US newspapers.

On July 22, 2014, Rezaian was arrested by Iranian authorities and charged with espionage (spying) and writing stories "against the establishment." Rezaian's trial was held behind closed doors, so no one knew how it was conducted. He was sentenced to prison, but Iran would not say how many years he would serve.

Fortunately, Jason Rezaian was released by the Iranians in early 2016. Still, his case serves as an example of what life might be like in a country without our Bill of Rights—and specifically, the First Amendment.

On September 23, 2014, Iranian activists protested in New York City about the lack of freedom of the press in Iran.

CHAPTER 2

WHAT IS "THE PRESS?"

TYPES OF "PRESS"

Colonial printers established newspapers as a sideline to their main printing business. The future Founding Father, Benjamin Franklin, was one of the earlier newspaper publishers. He and his colleagues played a central role in publicizing the American Revolution. For hundreds of years, the only press in America was its newspapers.

RADIO

That changed in 1920 when KDKA in Pittsburgh, Pennsylvania, became the nation's first commercially licensed radio station. The military had already been using radio waves to communicate with one another, as had some private individuals. KDKA, however, broadcast its programs to the broader, general public. Many early radio stations were started by newspapers concerned about losing out to the new technology. Like today's radio stations, KDKA made money by selling airtime to advertisers. It also created a new kind of journalist: the radio news reporter.

These people are listening to an early radio broadcast, around 1925.

TELEVISION

In 1928, the world changed once again. The television station W2XB made its first broadcast in Schenectady, New York. New media professions were born: television news anchors, video photographers, and reporters, who could both cover the news and appear live on the air.

Early television equipment, dating from about 1930, shows a viewing mirror that reflects the image of an encased picture tube, with camera and transmission devices in the background.

Fast Fact

WARREN G. HARDING

KDKA made its first broadcast on November 2, 1920. It reported the results of the presidential contest between Warren G. Harding (pictured here) and James M. Cox. Interestingly, both men were newspaper publishers before running for political office. Harding was the 29th president of the United States (1921–1923).

THE DEFINITION OF "THE PRESS" EXPANDS

In 1938, Alma Lovell was arrested for spreading religious pamphlets in Griffin, Georgia. The town had an ordinance prohibiting the distribution of leaflets and other materials without obtaining written permission from the City Manager. Lovell **appealed** her conviction on First Amendment grounds, saying the city's policy violated press protections, even though she wasn't distributing a "newspaper." The case made its way through the court system until it reached the highest court in the land: the Supreme Court of the United States.

The US Supreme Court is the highest court in the land, and it hears appeals only from lower courts, generally on topics it considers to be of national significance. It chooses just a small number of appeals to hear each year. As the supreme appellate court of the entire country, its decisions are final. No other court can overturn a Supreme Court decision.

The Supreme Court agreed with Lovell. In the Court's **opinion**, the press consisted of not just magazines and newspapers. Rather, it included every sort of publication that acts as a vehicle for information and opinion. This definition eventually expanded to include plays, books, blogs, podcasts, and even video games.

BROWN V. ENTERTAINMENT MERCHANTS ASSOCIATION

In 2005, California passed a law prohibiting the sale of violent video games to children unless their parents granted permission. Although a ratings system for video games (like that for movies) was created in 1994, legislators in California felt additional protections were required.

The California legislature attempted to outlaw the sale of violent video games such as this.

THE CHALLENGE

The Entertainment Merchants Association, whose members sold video games, challenged the law and won. Then-governor Arnold Schwarzenegger vowed to fight the ruling. He took the case all the way to the Supreme Court. In a 7–2 decision, the Supreme Court justices struck down the California law.

In the Court's opinion, Justice Antonin Scalia wrote: "Like the protected books, plays, and movies that preceded them, video games communicate ideas—and even social messages—through many familiar literary devices (such as characters, dialogue, plot, and music) and through features distinctive to the medium (such as the player's interaction with the virtual world). That suffices to confer First Amendment protection."

Fast Fact

★ ★ ★ ★

ANTONIN SCALIA

Antonin Scalia died in February 2016 at the age of 79. Scalia was appointed to the Supreme Court in 1986 and served for nearly 30 years (10,732 days) as Supreme Court justice. But he ranks only number 15 by length of term of justices. In first place is William O. Douglas, who served 13,358 days between 1939 and 1975.

ADVERTISING AND THE PRESS

Flip through any newspaper, magazine, or website. What do you see? Certainly, there are articles and photographs. But there are also advertisements, and they, too, receive First Amendment protection.

THE NEW YORK TIMES

In 1964, *The New York Times* ran a full-page ad seeking to raise money to defend civil rights leader Martin Luther King Jr. against charges of lying under oath. In the ad, several incorrect statements were made with regard to the Montgomery, Alabama, police department. The police chief sued the newspaper for **defamation**. He won his case in an Alabama court, but *The New York Times* appealed.

The New York Times is one of the leading US daily newspapers. It was founded in 1851 and is regarded by many as the "newspaper of record." The newspaper is located in midtown Manhattan in New York City.

MALICE

When the defamation case reached the Supreme Court, the justices decided that the false statements were not made on purpose. In other words, there was no "actual malice"—bad intent—on the *Times*'s part. Without malice, the Court ruled, there could be no defamation. The Supreme Court therefore reversed the Alabama state court's decision. This remains a **landmark** case and one that made "actual malice" a requirement in order to prove libel.

OPINION VERSUS REPORTING

Parody is one way of stating an opinion. It can take the form of a written piece, or it can be a song, cartoon, costume, sculpture, or some other type of art. A parody imitates another work, while at the same time creating a new message. Like other forms of communication, it is protected by the First Amendment.

In February 2016, demonstrators used figures of presidential candidates Donald Trump and Hillary Clinton holding bags of money, with "Mr. Monopoly" behind them, to highlight the role of money in politics.

DAMAGES

By the 1980s, the question before the Supreme Court was whether or not a well-known person could seek **damages** for a parody published in a national magazine. The individual in question was a widely recognized minister who regularly appeared on television. The parody was based on a liquor ad. Among other things, it depicted the pastor as a drunkard. Even though the magazine added the line "ad parody—not to be taken seriously," the minister believed the ad to be libelous. The Supreme Court ruled against the pastor on the ground that the magazine never assumed its readers would believe the parody to be true.

Fast Fact

★ ★ ★ ★
WEIRD AL YANKOVIC

While some parodies are unflattering, Weird Al Yankovic's creations are funny songs meant only to entertain. Although he is not legally bound to do so, Yankovic asks performers' permission before parodying their music. Two of his best known parodies are "Eat It" (after Michael Jackson's "Beat It") and "Living with a Hernia" (after James Brown's "Living in America").

CHAPTER 3

THE ROLE OF THE PRESS

NEWS EVERYWHERE

Today, news is broadcast over a variety of platforms including social media, websites, video sharing services, print and digital publications, radio, and television. The topics on which the media reports depend on the audience. For instance, a magazine might target a specific "special interest" group—people interested in only one issue or subject. A blog might seek to reach residents of one specific town. Large media outlets work to attract a widespread, or general, audience. Whoever the readers or viewers are, the job of the media is to provide a free flow of information and opinion.

A magazine or website on cats might target animal lovers.

NEWS ON THE GO

Armed with facts from objective news stories, the public can make better decisions. Voters, for example, can learn the views of opposing political candidates. During natural disasters, the nation turns to the media to learn how to stay safe. In 1990, weather forecasters could provide only a five-minute warning before a tornado touched down. Today, this critical period has increased to 15 minutes—often enough time for **meteorologists** to alert residents to take shelter. In these instances, the media helps save lives.

Of course, not all news stories involve such serious subject matter. Some reporters cover more light-hearted topics, such as celebrity news or sports. The press not only informs and educates, but it also entertains.

With the ability to carry news around with you, there is little excuse for today's citizens to be uninformed.

THE PRESS AS GOVERNMENT WATCHDOG

Because the government has such a large impact on our lives, reporters spend a great deal of time covering it. Your hometown newspaper probably writes many stories about city council or county commissioner meetings. Your local radio station might spend a great deal of time talking about the governor of your state. National television networks usually concentrate on the federal government. This includes the men and women who make our laws, the nation's courts, and the president.

In addition to elected officials and the **judiciary**, the media also monitors government agencies. Utility commissions, for instance, control the price of electricity, or decide how much your cable company can charge. Without a free press to report about these agencies, how would we know if they were doing their jobs—or abusing their power?

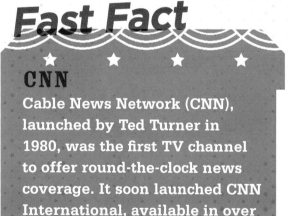

Fast Fact

CNN

Cable News Network (CNN), launched by Ted Turner in 1980, was the first TV channel to offer round-the-clock news coverage. It soon launched CNN International, available in over 200 countries worldwide.

NEWS AND THE ECONOMY

The news media also keeps an eye on the nation's financial health. The American economy is the largest in the world. That means we make and sell more products and services than any other nation. Thanks to our free press, Americans (and other countries who do business with us) know whether we are growing or in **recession**. This is important information when making investment and purchasing decisions.

Economic and business news is an important part of modern media, whether broadcast, print, or online.

SAFEGUARDING PUBLIC WELL-BEING

The press covers an infinite variety of important and interesting topics. It can be argued that no stories are as important as those involving public health and well-being.

Protecting our environment is of great concern to the public. Catastrophes such as oil and chemical spills can destroy wildlife and affect air and water quality. By reporting these mishaps, the media educates the public, which in turn can lead citizens to force companies and government agencies to clean up such disasters as quickly as possible.

Media reports of environmental disasters, such as the BP oil spill of 2010, often lead to public demands for action. This image shows sludge from that event on the beaches at Gulf Shores, Alabama.

★ ★ ★ ★ ★ ★ ★ ★

DEEPWATER HORIZON OIL SPILL

In 2010, the BP-owned oil rig *Deepwater Horizon* exploded and sank in the Gulf of Mexico. Nearly 5 million barrels of oil leaked into the ocean. Photographs and video of oil-coated wildlife and beaches angered the nation. As a result, both the US government and BP faced great pressure to stop the leak and clean up the spill.

FLINT, MICHIGAN

A recent case concerning water contamination proves that journalists aid in improving living conditions. In 2014, the people of Flint, Michigan, noticed something wrong with their drinking water. Scientists eventually discovered it contained large amounts of lead. State agencies were accused of covering up their knowledge of the problem. Massive press coverage of the crisis spurred Michigan officials to upgrade Flint's water delivery system and replace the old lead pipes that were creating the health problems.

CHAPTER 4

LIMITS ON FREEDOM OF THE PRESS

WHAT ARE THOSE LIMITS?

While the First Amendment guarantees that the press can generally operate without fear of punishment, there are limits to how the media can gather news and what they can report and publish. For example, writing aimed at illegally overthrowing the United States government is prohibited. Such an overthrow would lead to anarchy, a state of lawlessness.

The press is also forbidden from encouraging an assassination or other criminal activity. Our nation has endured the killing of four presidents: Lincoln, Garfield, McKinley, and Kennedy. However, our Constitution provides for the orderly transfer of power between governments. If the press began to encourage the assassination of our leaders, peace and order would clearly be threatened.

President Abraham Lincoln was assassinated by John Wilkes Booth at Ford's Theatre in Washington, DC, on April 14, 1865.

NATIONAL SECURITY COMES FIRST

It is unlawful for the press to share national secrets or print stories that endanger national security. If they do, they can be found guilty of espionage or even treason, which means betraying your own country. However, arguments frequently arise between the press and the government about what information should be released, and what should be kept secret—in short, who decides what information is **classified** and what is not.

In 2010, US Army Private Bradley Manning was arrested for sharing more than 700,000 documents and videos on the wars in Iraq and Afghanistan with a website called WikiLeaks. Though not the actual publisher of the information, Manning was **court-martialed** by the US Army and was sentenced to 35 years in prison.

In June 2013, protesters in San Francisco demanded freedom for Private Bradley Manning.

Fast Fact

WIKILEAKS

WikiLeaks is an international media organization founded in 2006 to publish censored and restricted documents from anonymous news sources and leaks. To date, it has published more than 10 million documents.

WikiLeaks's founder is Julian Assange. The self-stated goal of his website is to "open governments" by publishing information it deems important to the public. Wanted in several countries, Assange found asylum in the Embassy of Ecuador in London. He has not yet been tried by the United States for the release of these classified materials.

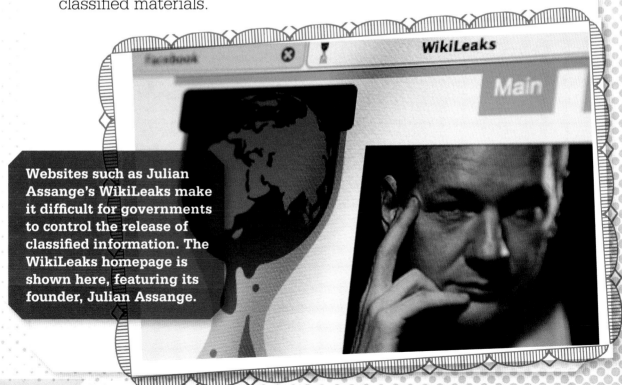

Websites such as Julian Assange's WikiLeaks make it difficult for governments to control the release of classified information. The WikiLeaks homepage is shown here, featuring its founder, Julian Assange.

SLANDER AND LIBEL

The press cannot publish or report information it knows to be false. False statements appearing in print are called libel, while untrue spoken statements are called slander. Dishonest claims can greatly harm an individual's personal or professional reputation.

THE COACHES SUE

In 1963, the *Saturday Evening Post* published an article implying that two football coaches—Paul "Bear" Bryant and James Wallace "Wally" Butts—**conspired** to fix a Georgia–Alabama game the previous year. The magazine's source for the article was George Burnett, an insurance salesman who supposedly overheard a telephone conversation between the two.

The coaches sued the magazine for making false statements damaging someone's reputation, known as defamation. Bryant eventually settled out of court for $300,000, but Butts pursued his case all the way to the Supreme Court. The justices found that the *Saturday Evening Post* failed to try to verify Burnett's claims before printing them. They ruled that Butts had indeed been defamed. Although he originally asked for $10 million in damages, Butts was eventually awarded only $460,000.

Fast Fact

THE SATURDAY EVENING POST

The Saturday Evening Post is an iconic American magazine. Founded in 1821, it attracted famous writers such as Edgar Allan Poe and F. Scott Fitzgerald. The artist Norman Rockwell became a household name thanks to his cover illustrations for the *Post*.

INVASION OF PRIVACY

For years, Americans have debated whether or not the US Constitution guarantees a right to privacy. Although privacy is not specifically defined in the Constitution, many believe it is implied by the Fourth Amendment's mention of the "right of the people to be secure in their persons, houses, papers, and effects." Although the First Amendment gives journalists and photographers the freedom to pursue newsworthy stories by legal means, they cannot trespass or invade an individual's privacy.

Photographers who specialize in taking pictures of celebrities are called "paparazzi." These paparazzi often go to extreme lengths to follow and photograph famous people. They then sell the photos to websites, newspapers, and magazines.

Some people think that the paparazzi was to blame for Princess Diana's death in a car crash in August 1997.

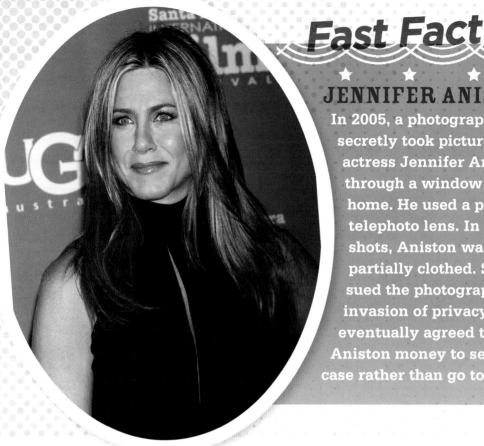

★ ★ ★ ★

JENNIFER ANISTON

In 2005, a photographer secretly took pictures of the actress Jennifer Aniston through a window of her home. He used a powerful telephoto lens. In some shots, Aniston was only partially clothed. She sued the photographer for invasion of privacy. He eventually agreed to pay Aniston money to settle the case rather than go to trial.

WHAT THE PRESS CANNOT DO

The press is guilty of invasion of privacy if reporters or photographers:

- Trespass on private property or peep into windows
- Use secretly placed cameras or illegal wiretaps to record personal, private activities
- Use false identities to trick people into giving them access to private or prohibited locations
- Print details that are offensive or non-newsworthy
- Use an individual's name or likeness, without permission, to make money

CHAPTER 5

CHALLENGES TO FREEDOM OF THE PRESS

REGULATIONS

Like other freedoms in the Bill of Rights, the First Amendment is often challenged. Sometimes the results of these challenges seem to contradict themselves.

Television and radio stations are governed by the Federal Communications Commission. In 1949, the FCC introduced a regulation called the "fairness doctrine." It required coverage to be split equally in the case of personal attacks—particularly when delivered during a political discussion. In 1969, the fairness doctrine was challenged in a lawsuit, but the Supreme Court found it to be constitutional.

The Federal Communications Commission headquarters is located in Washington, DC.

Ironically, in 1987, the FCC voluntarily eliminated the fairness doctrine. A provision called the "equal-time rule"—which dictates that political opponents who request it receive equal radio and television coverage—is still in effect in certain circumstances.

Fast Fact

SATURDAY NIGHT LIVE AND NBC

During the 2016 presidential campaign, two candidates appeared on the comedy show *Saturday Night Live*. NBC sent memos to its local affiliates detailing the exact number of minutes and seconds these individuals appeared, in the event that other political candidates demanded equal time. The NBC Studios (shown here) are located at 30 Rockefeller Center in New York City.

NEWSPAPERS

While radio and television stations are bound by equal-time requirements, the Supreme Court takes a seemingly conflicting stance regarding newspapers. In the 1970s, Pat Tornillo ran for election to Florida's House of Representatives. During the campaign, several **editorials** critical of Tornillo ran in the *Miami Herald*. A Florida state law required equal space for political content. Based on this law, Tornillo demanded equal space in the newspaper to respond. The *Herald* denied his request.

Tornillo sued. The case started in a county circuit court and was eventually appealed to Florida's Supreme Court. Finally, his case was reviewed by the Supreme Court of the United States. It ruled that by demanding newspaper editors to publish content against their will, Florida was violating the press protections guaranteed by the First Amendment.

For many, the Tornillo case established the idea that newspapers are the most protected medium in the nation.

UNLAWFUL ATTEMPTS TO SILENCE THE PRESS

Sometimes limiting media coverage serves a larger and protected purpose. For example, classified information benefiting our nation's enemies should not be published. Certain details of crimes are kept secret to aid investigators in identifying the guilty parties. But there have also been attempts to silence the press for purely personal reasons.

A TAXING MATTER

Huey Long was the governor of Louisiana from 1928 to 1932. A flamboyant politician, Long was particularly popular among the rural population of his state. Those in larger cities, however, were not as supportive. The largest newspapers in the state were in these cities, and they were often critical of Long. Long's administration passed a tax on publications with circulations of 20,000 or more readers. Coincidentally, this tax applied to those newspapers least friendly to the governor.

Huey Long was an American politician who battled newspapers in his home state of Louisiana that were critical of him.

Nine publishers filed a lawsuit against the tax. They argued that it was clearly aimed at throttling the press. The Supreme Court agreed with the publishers. In its written opinion, the Court reminded both parties that, for years, the British attempted to **abridge** freedom of expression in the American colonies. The tax, as imposed by the Long administration, acted in the same manner. It was therefore found to violate the First Amendment right to a free press.

THE PENTAGON PAPERS

In 1971, *The New York Times* published portions of a classified report known as the Pentagon Papers. This report gave the history of the United States' involvement in the Vietnam War between the years 1945 and 1967. It indicated that America had secretly expanded its efforts into the bordering countries of Cambodia and Laos.

A Vietnamese soldier motions to a woman refugee to keep her children's heads down during a fight with Viet Cong in January 1966.

The public was outraged that this information had been hidden from them. The US Department of Justice asked for and received a restraining order against the *Times*, which meant its journalists could no longer report on the story. The government claimed that publication of the Pentagon Papers endangered national security. The *Times* countered by saying it had a right to publish information helpful to the public's understanding of their government's policies.

The Supreme Court agreed with the newspaper. In its opinion, publishing the contents of this report did not threaten the safety of American forces. Barring its publication would, therefore, violate the freedom of the press.

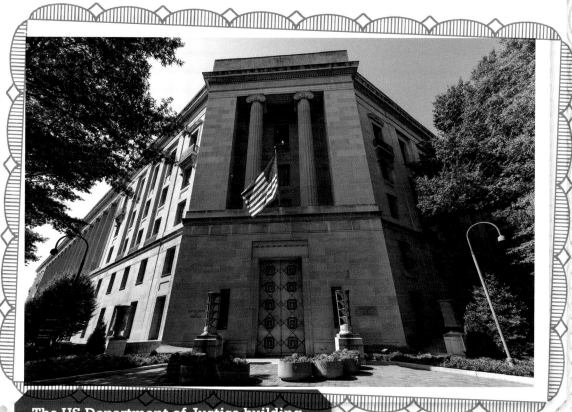

The US Department of Justice building is located in Washington, DC.

THE FIRST AMENDMENT AND STUDENT JOURNALISTS

In 1983, the students of Hazelwood East High School in Missouri wrote and edited a newspaper called *The Spectrum*. Two articles were set to appear in the newspaper: one dealing with divorce, the other with teen pregnancy. The school principal ordered that these stories be removed prior to publication. The student journalists, who included Cathy Kuhlmeier, sued on First Amendment grounds.

A student journalist interviews John Benetti, the principal of Union City High School in Union City, New Jersey, in March 2013. The occasion was a book signing by Professor David L. Kirp, whose book, *Improbable Scholars*, examines the successes of Union City's educational system.

RIGHTS VERSUS CENSORSHIP

The first court to hear the case agreed with the principal. But Kuhlmeier appealed that decision and won. The school then appealed to the US Supreme Court, which determined that it was within the rights of a school to eliminate stories it deemed inappropriate. There was, the Court decided, no breach of the student journalists' First Amendment rights because the newspaper was published by the school with public funds.

Fast Fact

★ ★ ★ ★ ★ ★
AFTER THE VERDICT

Years after the verdict, Kuhlmeier told audiences that the Supreme Court's ruling in favor of Hazelwood East High took too much power from students.

CHAPTER 6
THE FUTURE OF THE PRESS

BLOGGING

Do you write a blog? Or do you read blogs written by others? Do you consider yourself or other blog writers to be members of the press? At least one federal judge agrees.

Crystal Cox, a self-proclaimed investigative blogger, wrote several stories about the Obsidian Finance Group. In one 2010 post, she accused the company and one of its founders of illegal activity. Obsidian sued Cox for defamation. Even though she did not write for a newspaper, television network, or other recognized media outlet, Cox considered herself a journalist. As such, she believed Obsidian had to show "actual malice" on her part to prove defamation. Her claims were rejected by the court.

Fast Fact

BLOGGING

A blog, or web log, is a log or record posted on the Internet. Many blogs are ongoing online journals or diaries, some with comments on particular subjects or themes. Blogs can be published by individuals or groups. MABs (multi-author blogs) are often established by mass media organizations such as TV networks or print or digital publishers. Most of those are professionally written, edited, and designed.

APPEAL

Cox appealed these decisions. A federal circuit court judge found her arguments compelling. In his opinion, Judge Andrew Hurwitz wrote that the protections of the First Amendment do not apply only to formally trained journalists and traditional news media. The difference between "the media" and others who write political or other commentary has become less clear due in large part to the Internet, Hurwitz noted. He reversed the lower court's judgments and ordered a new trial for Cox.

Reaction to the decision was mixed. Some viewed it as a win for freedom of the press. Others feel that, by allowing anyone to become a journalist simply by claiming to be, it weakens the profession.

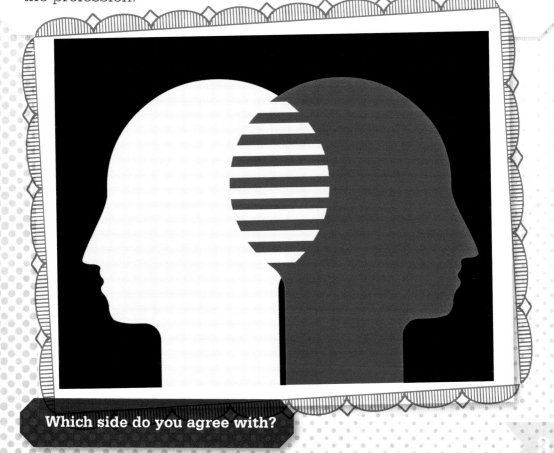

Which side do you agree with?

ARE YOU NEWSWORTHY?

Today we are not just asking "Who is the media?" We are also asking "What is news?"

Is your life newsworthy? Do reporters and photographers have a right to disclose your actions and habits? These are important questions in a world where everyone seems to have a camera and a social media account.

In 1999, US marshals and police officers from Montgomery County, Maryland, attempted to arrest the son of Charles and Geraldine Wilson. Two reporters from the *Washington Post* accompanied the officers on the arrest.

When they arrived at the Wilson home in the early hours of the morning, the police found Charles (wearing only boxer shorts) and Geraldine (clad only in her nightgown). The Wilsons' son was not present. Charles Wilson was subdued by the officers and forced to the floor. As this event unfolded, the *Washington Post* photographer took pictures.

Should photographers have the right to take anyone's picture, or are we entitled to privacy?

LAWSUIT

The Wilsons filed suit against Montgomery County, claiming that their constitutional right to privacy had been infringed by the officers. They also questioned why reporters were invited into their home to photograph these events. Police claimed the practice of allowing reporters to ride along on arrests was protected by the First Amendment.

The case reached the Supreme Court, which ruled in favor of the Wilsons. The Court found that the Fourth Amendment right to privacy trumped the right of the press (or any other third party) to be present during the execution of an arrest warrant. Still, the case raised many concerns.

Was what happened in the Wilson home newsworthy? Did reporters have a right to observe police executing an arrest warrant? Perhaps more importantly, in an increasingly digital world, how do we regulate what can and cannot be filmed or photographed?

Is it acceptable to take pictures of a concert or other live performance?

THE FOUNDING FATHERS AND THE INTERNET

In the 1700s, publishers probably assumed newspapers would be read and tossed away. Today, news stories live on indefinitely on the Internet. Does this mean that the First Amendment is less valid or applicable in our modern lives?

The truth is, "the press" is not just newspapers, and it never has been. When Thomas Paine authored his 1776 pamphlets encouraging Americans to declare independence from Britain, he was employing the power of the press. So, too, were the antislavery crusaders who created posters and published voting guides.

This statue, in Morristown, New Jersey, shows Thomas Paine writing his famous *Common Sense* pamphlet advocating freedom from Great Britain.

VIETNAM WAR PROTESTERS

When Vietnam War protesters wrote songs, poems, and books, they were using methods of communication the Supreme Court has declared are forms of the press.

While the Founding Fathers may never have expected news stories to live forever, they did devise a law to ensure that the press would. However, it is unlikely that publishers in colonial days ever imagined twenty-first-century students would be reading their newspapers!

JOHN LENNON AND PROTEST SONGS

John Lennon (1940–1980) was a British singer-songwriter who co-founded the Beatles around 1960. He then went on a decade later to launch a solo career. He wrote several protest songs, some of which became anthems of the antiwar movement. These included "Imagine" and "Give Peace a Chance," with the famous refrain, "All we are saying is give peace a chance."

CHAPTER 7

CONCLUSION

THE FORESIGHT OF THE FOUNDING FATHERS

In the United States, the press can be commercial (supported by advertising revenue), or it can be public (supported by donations and government funding). Courts have determined that the press includes journalists with college degrees, bloggers who consider themselves "citizen journalists," photographers, videographers, meteorologists, political cartoonists, playwrights, video game creators, and anyone else disseminating information and opinions.

Each one of us has a right to publish our thoughts, findings, and facts without fear of punishment by the government. This is one characteristic that distinguishes the United States from many other countries around the globe.

Reporters ask the questions the American public might ask if they had the access and opportunity. They sometimes pay for this curiosity with their lives.

Amos Doolittle's political cartoon *The Looking Glass for 1787* satirized the rival factions of business and agriculture on the eve of the ratification of the US Constitution. Such cartoons are also a form of press.

WHAT'S NEXT?

In 1799—eight years after the First Amendment was ratified—
Thomas Jefferson wrote: "I am for the freedom of the press, and
against all violations of the Constitution to silence by force and
not by reason the complaints or criticisms, just or unjust, of our
citizens against the conduct of their agents."

Thomas Jefferson, seen here in
about 1800, was mercilessly attacked
by the press during his presidency
(1801–1809), but he never wavered
in his support of a free press.

GLOSSARY

abridge—to cut short or curtail

Alien and Sedition Acts of 1798—laws making it illegal to protest the government, in speech or in print

appeal—request for review by a higher court

classified—information designated as secret

conspire—to plan an unlawful act with others

court-martial—a trial in a military court

damages—the money that a person bringing a lawsuit might be paid

defamation—false statements that hurt an individual's reputation

editorial—an opinion piece written by the editor of a publication

judiciary—the court system

landmark—an event that marks an important change

meteorologist—someone who studies the atmosphere to forecast the weather

opinion—a written explanation of a court's decision

parody—a piece of writing that imitates another writer's style in an amusing way

ratification—confirmation or approval

recession—a period during which the economy weakens rather than grows

FURTHER INFORMATION

Books

Berkin, Carol. *The Bill of Rights: The Fight to Secure America's Liberties*. New York: Simon & Schuster, 2015.

Dooling, Sandra. *James Madison*. New York: Rosen Publishing, 2013.

Keegan, Anna. *The United States Constitution and the Bill of Rights*. New York: Rosen Publishing, 2016.

Krull, Kathleen. *A Kids' Guide to America's Bill of Rights*. New York: HarperCollins, 2015.

Online

Bill of Rights Institute
www.billofrightsinstitute.org/founding-documents/bill-of-rights/

Britannica.com, "Bill of Rights"
www.britannica.com/topic/Bill-of-Rights-United-States-Constitution

Cornell University Law School, Legal Information Institute
www.lawcornell.edu/constitution/billofrights

Publisher's note to educators and parents: Our editors have carefully reviewed these websites to ensure that they are suitable for students. Many websites change frequently, however, and we cannot guarantee that a site's future contents will continue to meet our high standards of quality and educational value. Be advised that students should be closely supervised whenever they access the Internet.

INDEX